Activity Books for Kids Ages 9 - 12
Mazes, Word Games, Puzzles & More! Hours of Fun!

Speedy Publishing LLC
40 E. Main St. #1156
Newark, DE 19711

www.SpeedyPublishing.Col

Copyright 2014
9781633839502
First Printed August 12, 2014

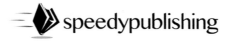

Boost your mind and creativity with these amazing activities that will challenge your brain.

Activity #1

Match the pairs:
find the exact mirror
copy for every picture.

*

Activity #2

Find the top view
for every stacking toy.

*

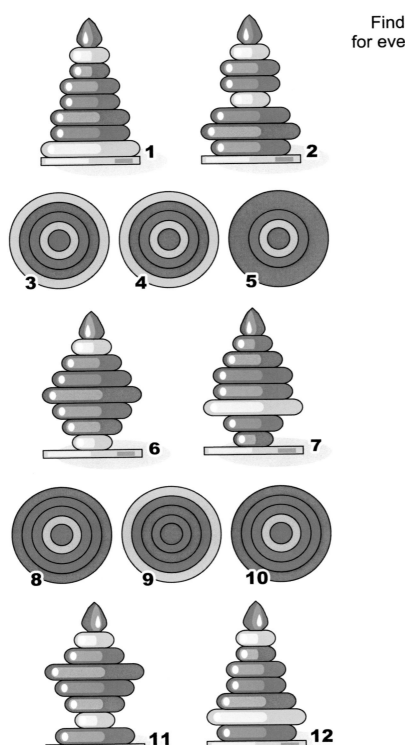

Activity #3

Which two pictures of the 6 are the exact mirror images of each other?

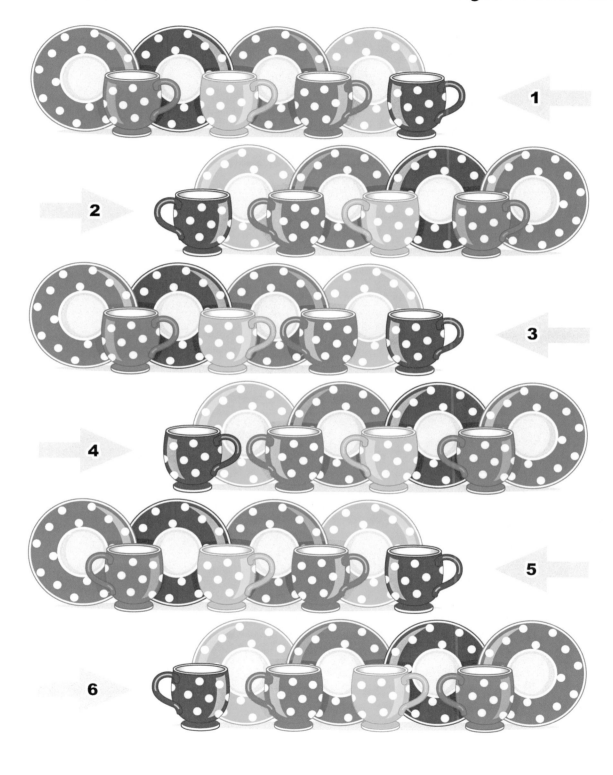

Activity #4

Match the halves
of picture cards.

Activity #5

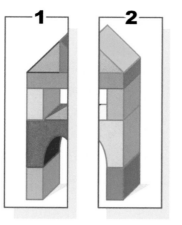 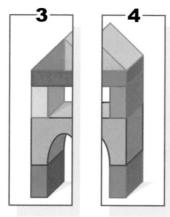

Match the halves
of picture cards.

*

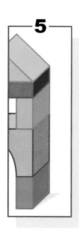 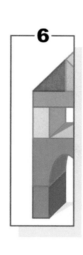 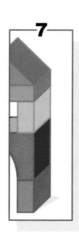 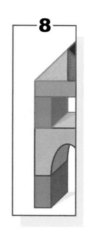

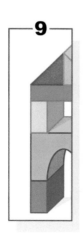 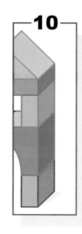 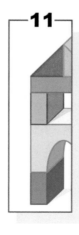 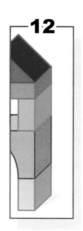

Activity #6

Match the halves
of picture cards.

*

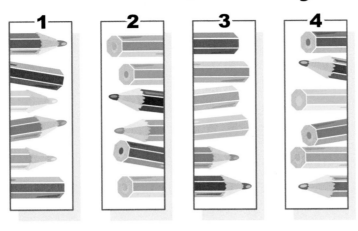

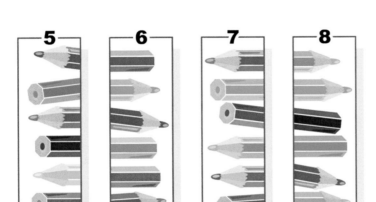

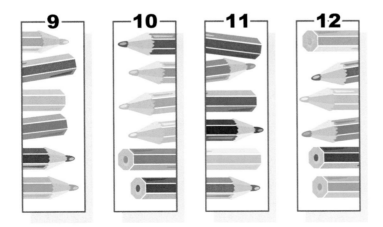

Activity #7

Find the bung
for each of the holes
in the lids of cans.

*

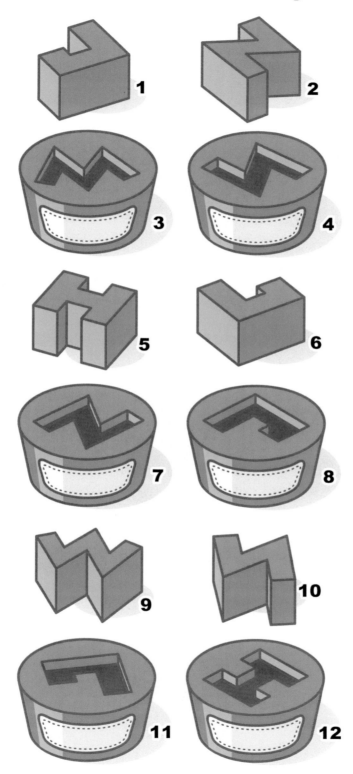

Activity #8

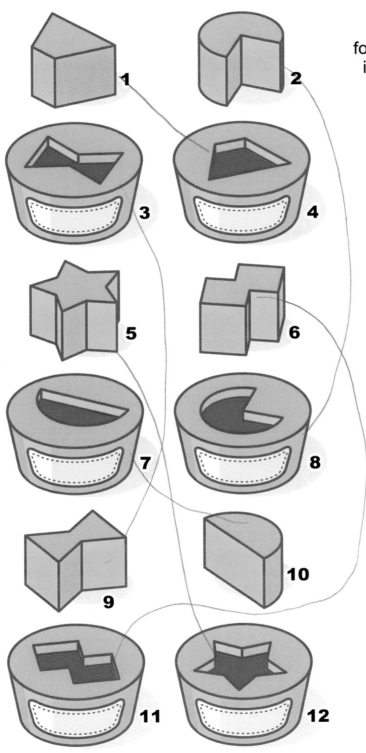

Find the bung
for each of the holes
in the lids of cans.

*

Activity #9

Match each fraction with its proper visual representation. (The numerators are represented by the red color.)

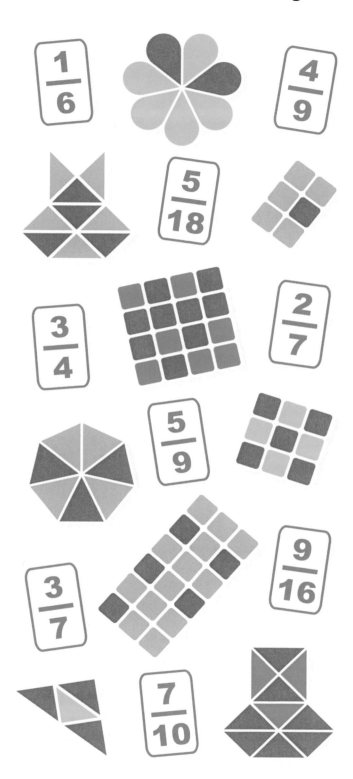

Activity #10

Match each fraction with its proper visual representation. (The numerators are represented by the red color.)

Activity #11

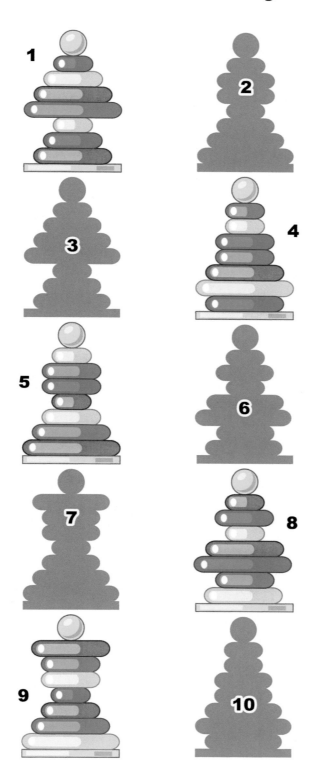

Match the pictures to their shadows.

*

Activity #12

Find the right piece
for each of these
cracked flower pots.

*

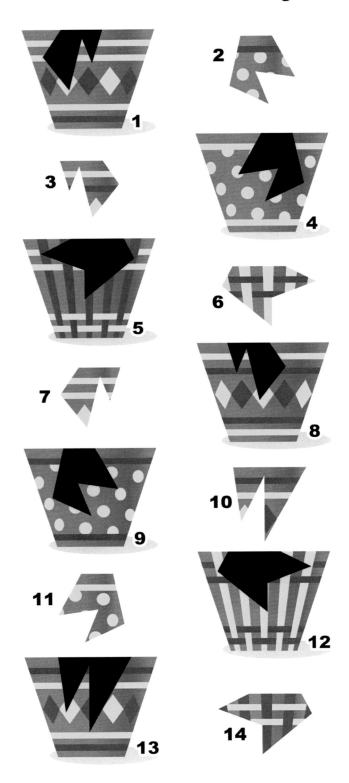

Activity #13

In every row remove just one matchstick to make the equation correct.

VI − I = VI

V + V = IX

XII − III = VIII

VI + V = I

IV − I = IV

IX + VIII = I

X − II = IX

15

Activity #14

1

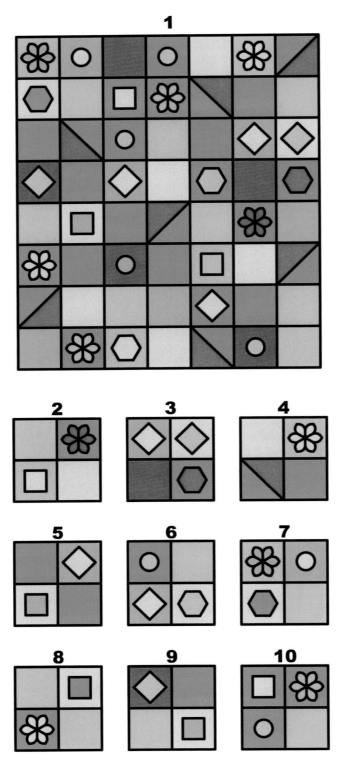

What of the 2 - 10
are not the fragments
of the picture 1?

*

2

3

4

5

6

7

8

9

10

Activity #15

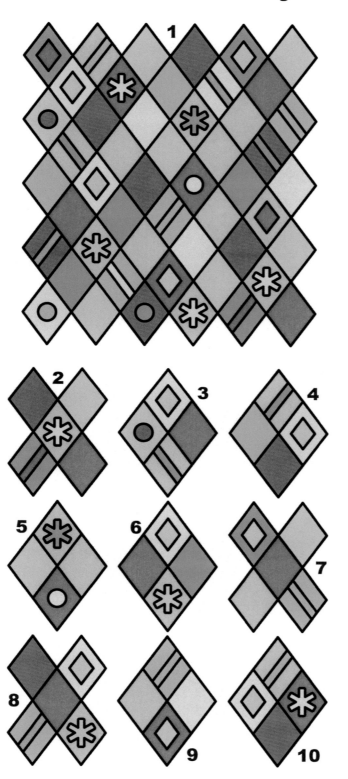

What of the 2 - 10
are not the fragments
of the picture 1?

*

Activity #16

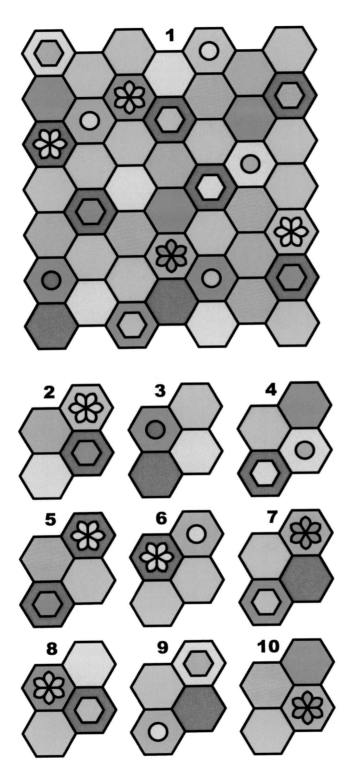

What of the 2 - 10
are not the fragments
of the picture 1?

*

18

Activity #17

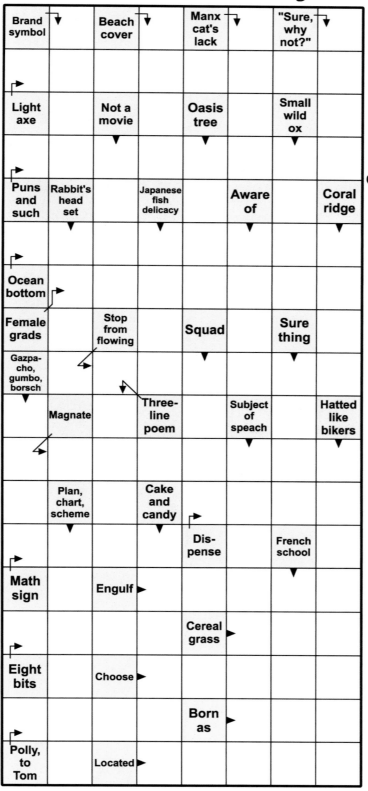

Clues-in-squares crossword puzzle, or arrow word puzzle, else arrowword.

To solve the puzzle simply write your answers in the direction of the arrows.

No unused squares. Squares with clues are highlighted.

Activity #18

Couple ▼	▼	Lofty ▼	▼	Rating unit ▼	▼	Spring flower ▼	▼
Flour box ▶		You're looking at it ▼		African cobras ▼		Way in, way out ▼	
Fruit farms ▶	Cave-man's weapon ▼		Part of a poem ▼		Clump ▼		Russo or Clair ▼
Artist, master of shapes ▶							
Spare time		Get some air		Mole-cule part ▼		Choir song ▼	
Food fish ▼	Clear soup		Update		Butter-fly ▼		Power of a number ▼
	Not here ▼		Hen tracks on paper ▼				
Furry feet ▶		Egypt's capital ▶	Celtic cat		Picture puzzle ▼		
			School tool ▶				
Mouse clicker ▶		Pueblo brick ▶					
			Sky shiner ▶				
Chilly powder		Mini-mum ▶					

Clues-in-squares crossword puzzle, or arrow word puzzle, else arrowword.

To solve the puzzle simply write your answers in the direction of the arrows.

No unused squares. Squares with clues are highlighted.

Activity #19

Fill in the blanks with the words ANT, CAN, CARD, KEY, KING, MALL, PEN, PIG, ROW, USE, WALL to unveil the names of eleven birds.

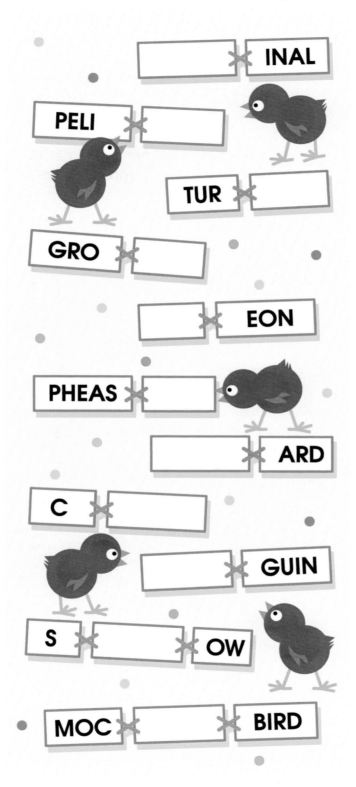

INAL

PELI

TUR

GRO

EON

PHEAS

ARD

C

GUIN

S   OW

MOC   BIRD

Activity #20

Fill in the blanks with the words AGE, ELECT, HIT, ICE, LEAN, MAN, OPERA, PEAK, PLUM, TAIL, URGE to reveal the names of 11 occupations (professions).

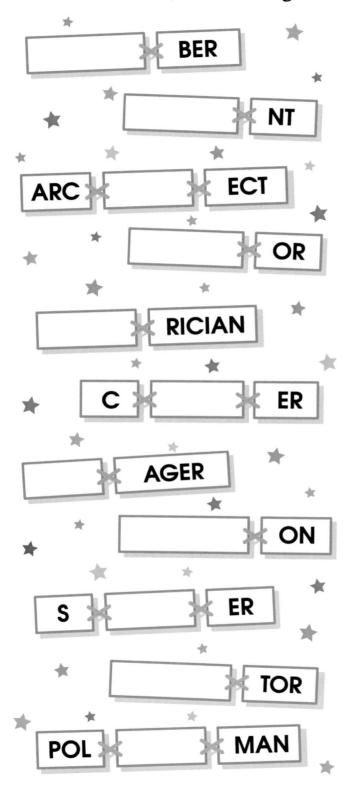

[____] **BER**

[____] **NT**

ARC [____] **ECT**

[____] **OR**

[____] **RICIAN**

C [____] **ER**

[____] **AGER**

[____] **ON**

S [____] **ER**

[____] **TOR**

POL [____] **MAN**

Activity #21

Words go left, right, up, down, not diagonaly, and can bend at a right angle. There are no unused letters in the grid, every letter is used only once.

Grid 1:

F	G	O	D	N	A	L	E	R	I
O	T	L	D	E	R	A	S	G	S
P	O	L	E	M	E	L	O	N	N
H	G	A	L	E	C	D	T	E	E
A	N	I	L	L	T	I	N	R	G
R	G	H	P	C	I	A	S	E	L
O	E	S	A	T	R	O	N	P	R
A	G	N	U	N	U	A	H	C	E
D	D	A	A	C	I	M	U	S	I
H	C	R	A	M	R	U	L	C	C

Word list 1:
- CELTIC
- CLAY PIPE
- CLOVER
- CLURICAUN
- DAGDA
- DANCES
- DRUIDS
- EMERALD
- GREEN
- HARP
- IRELAND
- KNOTWORK
- LEPRECHAUN
- MARCH
- MUSIC

Word list 2:
- ORANGE
- PARADE
- PATRON SAINT
- POETRY
- POT OF GOLD
- RAINBOW
- SERPENTS
- SHAMROCK
- SHILLELAGH
- SHOEMAKER
- SONGS
- TOP HAT
- TREFOIL
- WHITE

Grid 2:

H	A	S	H	O	E	M	E	P	A
C	R	P	R	E	K	A	D	A	R
L	A	E	P	C	L	O	V	E	R
D	Y	P	I	Y	R	T	E	O	P
A	N	T	R	E	F	O	I	L	W
K	C	E	S	W	H	D	R	U	O
N	S	E	S	H	I	S	D	I	B
O	P	R	S	A	T	T	H	A	N
T	E	N	T	M	E	O	P	T	I
W	O	R	K	R	O	C	K	R	A

23

Activity #22

Words go left, right, up, down, not diagonaly, and can bend at a right angle. There are no unused letters in the grid, every letter is used only once.

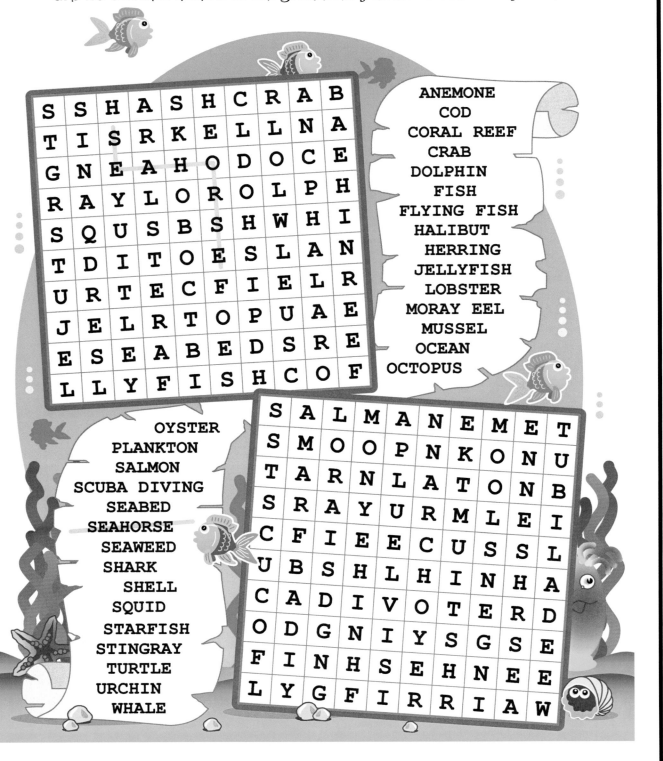

Grid 1:

S	S	H	A	S	H	C	R	A	B
T	I	S	R	K	E	L	L	N	A
G	N	E	A	H	O	D	O	C	E
R	A	Y	L	O	R	O	L	P	H
S	Q	U	S	B	S	H	W	H	I
T	D	I	T	O	E	S	L	A	N
U	R	T	E	C	F	I	E	L	R
J	E	L	R	T	O	P	U	A	E
E	S	E	A	B	E	D	S	R	E
L	L	Y	F	I	S	H	C	O	F

Word list (right):
ANEMONE
COD
CORAL REEF
CRAB
DOLPHIN
FISH
FLYING FISH
HALIBUT
HERRING
JELLYFISH
LOBSTER
MORAY EEL
MUSSEL
OCEAN
OCTOPUS

Word list (left):
OYSTER
PLANKTON
SALMON
SCUBA DIVING
SEABED
SEAHORSE
SEAWEED
SHARK
SHELL
SQUID
STARFISH
STINGRAY
TURTLE
URCHIN
WHALE

Grid 2:

S	A	L	M	A	N	E	M	E	T
S	M	O	O	P	N	K	O	N	U
T	A	R	N	L	A	T	O	N	B
S	R	A	Y	U	R	M	L	E	I
C	F	I	E	E	C	U	S	S	L
U	B	S	H	L	H	I	N	H	A
C	A	D	I	V	O	T	E	R	D
O	D	G	N	I	Y	S	G	S	E
F	I	N	H	S	E	H	N	E	E
L	Y	G	F	I	R	R	I	A	W

24

Activity #23
FILL-IN (or CRISS-CROSS) CROSSWORD PUZZLE

Fill in the blanks of the both grids with the words (ignore spaces and dashes):

(10) FREELANCER	(7) DOSSIER	(6) OLINDA	(5) CRANE	(5) PANDA	(4) ETNA
(10) INGREDIENT	(7) OCTOPUS	(6) PENCIL	(5) CYCLE	(5) RECAP	(4) MAIL
(10) KNIGHTHOOD	(7) SCREWER	(6) REBOOT	(5) EAGLE	(5) REEFS	(4) MAZE
(10) LITERATURE	(7) VICOMTE	(6) SCROLL	(5) ENTER	(5) REIKI	(4) NEST
(10) MANUSCRIPT	(6) ACROSS	(6) SENTRY	(5) ETHER	(5) TANGO	(4) NIGH
(10) RECREATION	(6) AIKIDO	(6) SPECIE	(5) EVENT	(5) TONER	(4) ODER
(10) ROADRUNNER	(6) APPEAR	(6) TIVOLI	(5) LEAST	(5) VICAR	(4) RARE
(10) SETTLEMENT	(6) DIVIDE	(6) UNIQUE	(5) LOTUS	(5) YACHT	(4) SLED
(7) CELESTE	(6) EDIBLE	(5) ARROW	(5) NOISE	(4) BOSC	
(7) CENTRAL	(6) ELIXIR	(5) CLOSE	(5) NORTH	(4) CRAB	
(7) COMPASS	(6) END RUN	(5) COCOA	(5) OKAPI	(4) CUBE	
(7) CRYSTAL	(6) NOTICE	(5) CORAL	(5) OPERA	(4) EARN	

Solutions

Activity #1

1 - 4,
2 - 8,
3 - 5,
6 - 7.

Activity #2

1 - 4,
2 - 10,
6 - 8,
7 - 9,
11 - 5,
12 - 3.

Activity #3

Which two pictures of the 6 are the exact mirror images of each other?

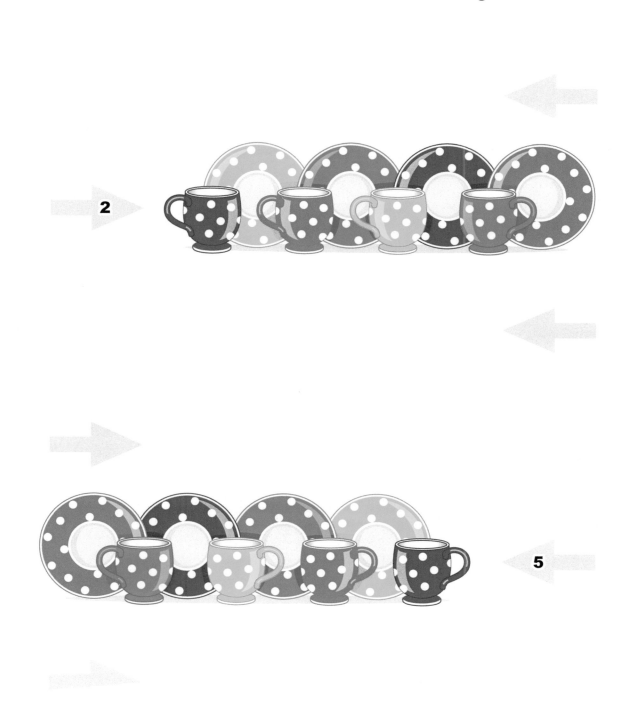

Activity #4

1 - 4
2 - 8,
3 - 10,
5 - 11,
6 - 12,
7 - 9.

Activity #5

1 - 7,
2 - 11,
3 - 5,
4 - 9,
6 - 10,
8 - 12.

Activity #6

1 - 4,
2 - 8,
3 - 10,
5 - 11,
6 - 7,
9 - 12.

Activity #7

3 - 9,
4 - 10,
7 - 2,
8 - 1,
11 - 6,
12 - 5.

Activity #8

3 - 9,
4 - 1,
7 - 10,
8 - 2,
11 - 6,
12 - 5.

Activity #10

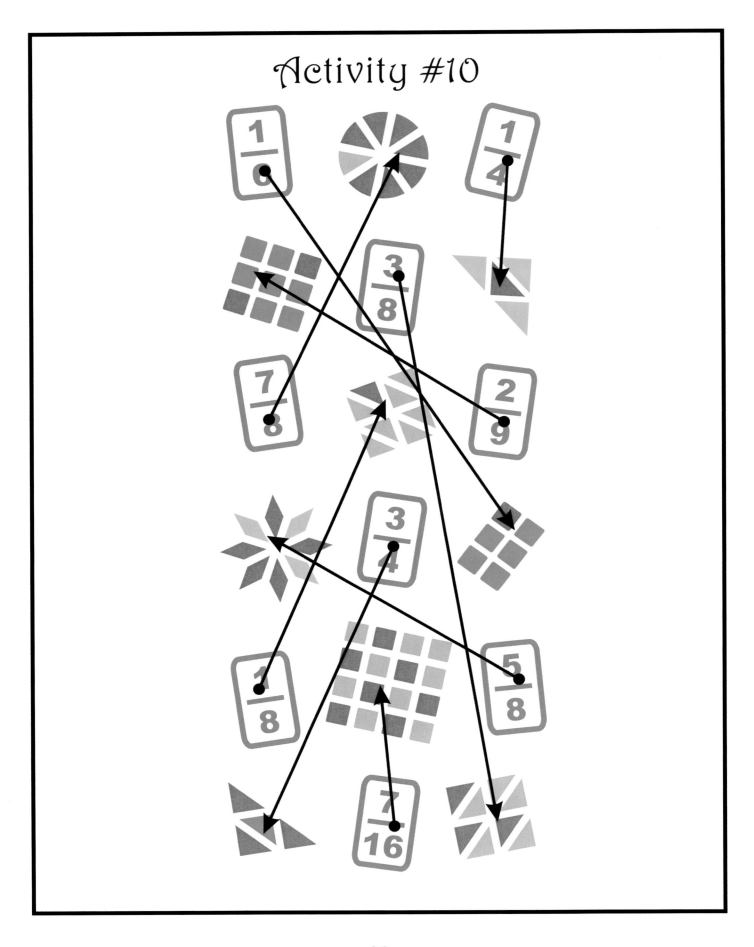

1 - 3,
4 - 10,
5 - 2,
8 - 6,
9 - 7.

**1 - 7,
4 - 11,
5 - 14,
8 - 3,
9 - 2,
12 - 6,
13 - 10.**

Activity #13

VI − I = V

V + V = X

XI − III = VIII

VI − V = I

V − I = IV

IX − VIII = I

X − I = IX

Activity #14

1

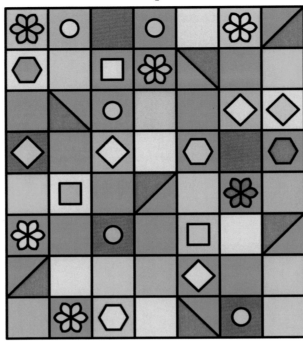

2

6

8

Activity #15

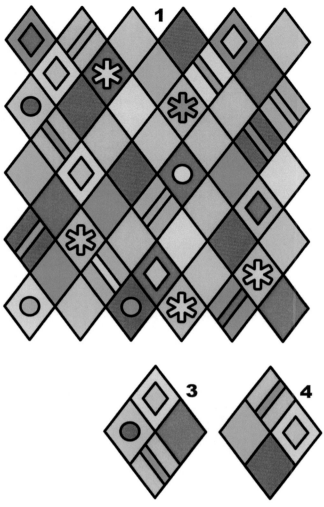

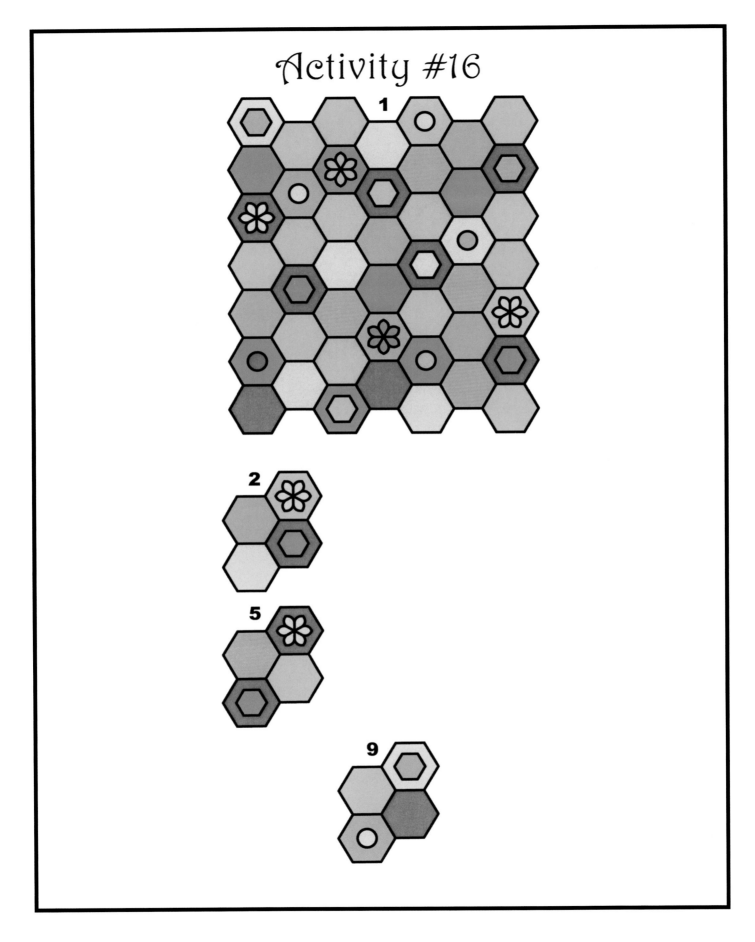

	L		S		T		O
T	O	M	A	H	A	W	K
	G		N		I		A
W	O	R	D	P	L	A	Y
		E		A		N	
S	E	A	F	L	O	O	R
	A	L	U	M	N	A	E
	R		G		T		E
	S	H	U	T	O	F	F
S		A		E		A	
O	L	I	G	A	R	C	H
U		K		M	E	T	E
P	L	U	S		F		L
	A		W	H	E	L	M
B	Y	T	E		R	Y	E
	O		E	L	E	C	T
A	U	N	T		N	E	E
	T		S	I	T	E	D

Activity #18

	P		H		S		I
C	A	N	I	S	T	E	R
	I		G		A		I
O	R	C	H	A	R	D	S
		L		S		O	
S	C	U	L	P	T	O	R
	L	E	I	S	U	R	E
	U		N		F		N
	B	R	E	A	T	H	E
S		E		T		Y	
C	O	N	S	O	M	M	E
U		E		M	A	N	X
P	A	W	S		R		P
	B		C	A	I	R	O
U	S	E	R		P	E	N
	E		A	D	O	B	E
S	N	O	W		S	U	N
	T		L	E	A	S	T

Activity #19

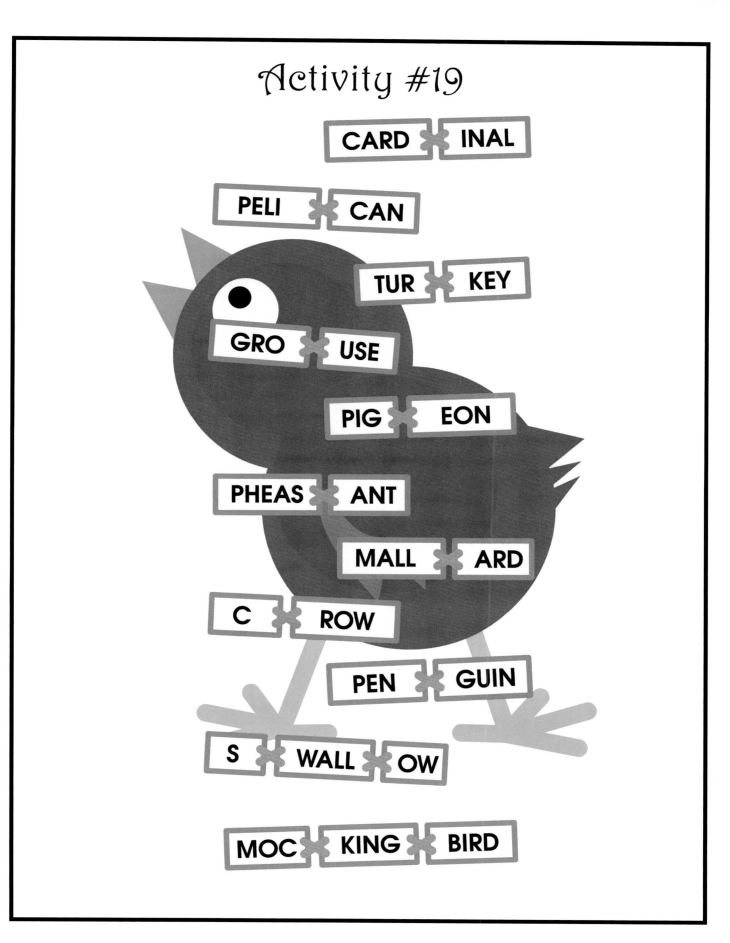

CARD ✕ INAL

PELI ✕ CAN

TUR ✕ KEY

GRO ✕ USE

PIG ✕ EON

PHEAS ✕ ANT

MALL ✕ ARD

C ✕ ROW

PEN ✕ GUIN

S ✕ WALL ✕ OW

MOC ✕ KING ✕ BIRD

Activity #20

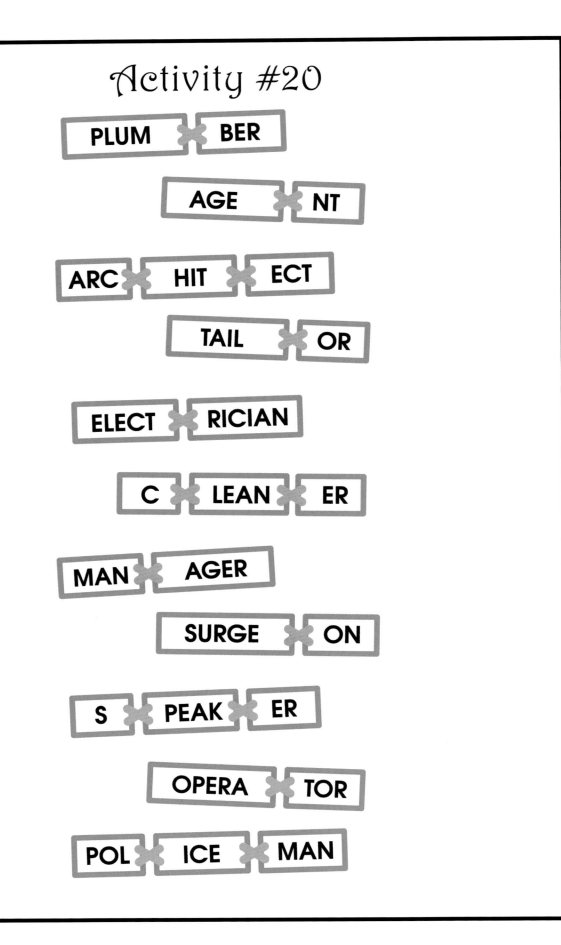

PLUM — BER

AGE — NT

ARC — HIT — ECT

TAIL — OR

ELECT — RICIAN

C — LEAN — ER

MAN — AGER

SURGE — ON

S — PEAK — ER

OPERA — TOR

POL — ICE — MAN

F	G	O	D	N	A	L	E	R	I
O	T	L	D	E	R	A	S	G	S
P	O	L	E	M	E	L	O	N	N
H	G	A	L	E	C	D	T	E	E
A	N	I	L	L	T	I	N	R	G
R	G	H	P	C	I	A	S	E	L
O	E	S	A	T	R	O	N	P	R
A	G	N	U	N	U	A	H	C	E
D	D	A	A	C	I	M	U	S	I
H	C	R	A	M	R	U	L	C	C

H	A	S	H	O	E	M	E	P	A
C	R	P	R	E	K	A	D	A	R
L	A	E	P	C	L	O	V	E	R
D	Y	P	I	Y	R	T	E	O	P
A	N	T	R	E	F	O	I	L	W
K	C	E	S	W	H	D	R	U	O
N	S	E	S	H	I	S	D	I	B
O	P	R	S	A	T	T	H	A	N
T	E	N	T	M	E	O	P	T	I
W	O	R	K	R	O	C	K	R	A

Activity #22

S	A	L	M	A	N	E	M	E	T
S	M	O	O	P	N	K	O	N	U
T	A	R	N	L	A	T	O	N	B
S	R	A	Y	U	R	M	L	E	I
C	F	I	E	E	C	U	S	S	L
U	B	S	H	L	H	I	N	H	A
C	A	D	I	V	O	T	E	R	D
O	D	G	N	I	Y	S	G	S	E
F	I	N	H	S	E	H	N	E	E
L	Y	G	F	I	R	R	I	A	W

S	S	H	A	S	H	C	R	A	B
T	I	S	R	K	E	L	L	N	A
G	N	E	A	H	O	D	O	C	E
R	A	Y	L	O	R	O	L	P	H
S	Q	U	S	B	S	H	W	H	I
T	D	I	T	O	E	S	L	A	N
U	R	T	E	C	F	I	E	L	R
J	E	L	R	T	O	P	U	A	E
E	S	E	A	B	E	D	S	R	E
L	L	Y	F	I	S	H	C	O	F

Activity #23

Grid 1:

R	E	C	R	E	A	T	I	O	N
A		R		A		A	P		P
R	O	A	D	R	U	N	N	E	R
E		B		N		G		R	
	S		R		C	O	R	A	L
A	P	P	E	A	R		E		O
	E		B		Y	A	C	H	T
A	C	R	O	S	S		A		U
	I		O	C	T	O	P	U	S
C	E	N	T	R	A	L		N	
R		O		E	L	I	X	I	R
A	R	R	O	W		N		Q	
N		T		E	N	D	R	U	N
E	T	H	E	R		A		E	
	O		A		E		B		O
K	N	I	G	H	T	H	O	O	D
	E		L		N		S		E
F	R	E	E	L	A	N	C	E	R

Grid 2:

M	A	N	U	S	C	R	I	P	T
A		I		L		E		A	
I	N	G	R	E	D	I	E	N	T
L		H		D		K		D	
	D		N		V	I	C	A	R
T	I	V	O	L	I		O		E
	V		T		C	Y	C	L	E
A	I	K	I	D	O		O		F
	D		C	O	M	P	A	S	S
C	E	L	E	S	T	E		C	
L		E		S	E	N	T	R	Y
O	K	A	P	I		C		O	
S		S		E	D	I	B	L	E
E	N	T	E	R		L		L	
	O		V		M		C		N
L	I	T	E	R	A	T	U	R	E
	S		N		Z		B		S
S	E	T	T	L	E	M	E	N	T